Time-to-Discover READERS
SCHOLASTIC

D0131908

Leaves

Melvin and Gilda Berger

SCHOLASTIC INC.
New York Toronto London Auckland Sydney
Mexico City New Delhi Hong Kong Buenos Aires

Photographs: Cover: George Ranalli/Photo Researchers;
p. 1: Bill Lea/DPA (Dembinsky Photo Associates);
p. 3: Raymond Gehman/Corbis; p. 4: Rod Planck/DPA; p. 5: Michael P. Gadomski/DPA;
p. 6: Sharon Cummings/DPA; p. 7: Darrell Gulin/Corbis; p. 8: Lon C. Diehl/PhotoEdit;
p. 9: Royalty-Free/Corbis; p. 10: Jim Zipp/Photo Researchers; p. 11: Dan Dempster/DPA;
p. 12: Burke/Triolo/Brand X Pictures/Picture Quest;
p. 13: Myrleen Ferguson Cate/PhotoEdit;
p. 14: Rod Planck/Photo Researchers; p. 15: Franc Müller/Okapia/Photo Researchers;
p. 16: Carola Koserowsky/Okapia/Photo Researchers.

Photo Research: Sarah Longacre

ISBN 0-439-67897-8

12 11 10 9 8 7 6 5 4 3 2 1   4 5 6 7 8 9/0

Printed in the U.S.A.
First Scholastic printing, September 2004

Leaves turn different colors in autumn.

Leaves turn yellow.

Leaves turn orange.

Leaves turn red.

Fun Fact

When leaves lose
their green color,
other colors
show through.

Leaves turn purple.

Days are rainy.

Fun Fact

Rain and wind knock some of the leaves from the trees.

Days are windy.

The leaves fall.

Fun Fact

Trees that lose their leaves in the fall are called deciduous (dih-SIJ-oo-uhs) trees.

They cover the ground.

Some leaves are big.

Fun Fact

Trees that do not lose their leaves in the fall are called evergreens.

Some leaves are small.

Some leaves are smooth.

Fun Fact
The edges of some leaves look like the blade on a saw.

Some leaves are pointy.

Leaves come in many colors, sizes, and shapes!